1. Introduction

Policymakers use estimates of labor supply elasticities to understand how tax changes affect labor supply and, by extension, tax revenues and economic growth. A number of researchers have estimated these elasticities on both the participation and hours margins. While many studies estimate elasticities close to zero for married men, estimated elasticities among married women have fallen dramatically over the last 40 years and now approach those of married men. The studies present various explanations for this trend—women's stronger attachment to the labor force, increasing levels of educational attainment, and smaller family sizes. These factors also have led to a higher labor force participation rate, which reduces the number of women who could potentially enter the labor force.

It is increasingly common for married women to be the primary earners in their families. The share of dual earner couples in which the wife earns more than her husband has increased from 19 percent in 1987 to 29 percent in 2012 (Bureau of Labor Statistics 2014). If couples in which the husband does not work are included, the share of couples in which the wife earns more has increased from 24 percent to 38 percent over that same time period. This change suggests another reason for the decline in wage elasticities of married women. If the secondary worker in a couple is less attached to the labor market than the primary earner, and women are now more likely to be the primary earner, then one would expect to see labor supply elasticities for married women to decline over time.

In this paper, we use data derived from a panel of tax returns to examine whether being the marginal worker in a couple (in the sense of having the larger labor supply elasticity) tends to be determined by that member's sex or by his or her relative earnings. Using stylized facts, we demonstrate that lower earning spouses transition into and out of the labor force more frequently than married women. Notably, this result does not hold if the couple starts a family. We then estimate participation elasticities with respect to the net-of-tax rate for women and secondary earners. This allows us to directly compare the results of women and secondary earners using the same data.

This paper makes several other contributions to the literature. First, participation elasticities have typically been estimated using survey data. Administrative tax return data can allow us to more accurately measure labor force participation and estimate the net-of-tax rate. Second, the panel aspect of this dataset allows us to observe how spouses transition into and out of the labor force, and to distinguish between the behavior of the higher and lower earners within the household. It also allows us to address the potential biases caused by unobserved heterogeneity. Third, although tax return data have been used to estimate the elasticity of income, our estimates provide additional information about whether changes in taxable income reflect changes in the secondary worker's labor force participation.

2. Literature Review

A large existing literature studies the sensitivity of labor supply to incentives such as the wage rate or the marginal tax rate. The estimated elasticities tend to be low, especially for hours worked. An exception is the elasticity for married women along the extensive margin, in which individuals choose to work or not work for pay. Estimates of those elasticities have historically been higher than for married or single men or single women. More recent estimates for married women are much lower, suggesting that married women are less frequently the marginal worker in a household, if a marginal worker exists. Several recent articles focus on the fact that wives are more frequently the primary earner in a couple, and that the relative earnings may play a role in determining whether or not an individual holds a paid position.

Blau and Kahn (2007) and Heim (2007) each describe the changes in female labor force participation from about 1980 through 2000. Blau and Kahn note that in the 1980s female labor supply rose independently of wages and that increase slowed in the 1990s. They observe that historically women's labor supply has been much more sensitive to wages than men's labor supply because traditional gender roles lead women to substitute among work, home production, and leisure while men substitute between work and leisure. But they point out that as traditional gender roles break down, women's cross-wage and wage elasticities would approach those of men. Using March Current Population Survey (CPS) data from 1980 through 2000, they estimate the wage and cross-wage elasticities of married women at different points in time. They find that married women's participation elasticities with respect to their own wages fell from a range of 0.53 to 0.61 in 1980 to a range of 0.27 to 0.30 in 2000, while elasticities over the intensive margin exhibited smaller declines. Heim (2007) also studies the decline in elasticities among married women using March CPS data from 1979 through 2003. He estimates the decline in estimated elasticities using a series of cross-sectional analyses. He concludes that hours and participation elasticities fell substantially over those years, with participation elasticities with respect to wages falling from 0.66 to 0.03.

Heim presents several explanations for the decline in estimated participation elasticities. First, women's average age of first marriage increased over the time period covered in the sample. That increase implies that more women have established careers before marrying, which could lead to women being more attached to the labor force towards the later years in the sample. Second, there has been a shift by women into occupations that have more stable hours and employment. Third, the increased risk of divorce may lead women to partially insure against that risk by maintaining continuous work histories that would help them obtain or continue employment after a divorce.

A few papers have examined the importance of relative earnings for labor supply decisions. Shafer (2011) demonstrates that the labor force participation decision of a woman is more closely linked to her income relative to her husband's income than it is to either of their incomes in isolation. Shafer's analysis uses the National Longitudinal Survey of Youth from 1979-2004 and focuses on women who were in the work force when they married. Using several different models, she shows that the wife's wages relative to her husband's better predicts an exit from the labor force than either her income or her husband's income. This result holds even after controlling for the possibility that women have low wages because they plan on exiting the labor force and so do not pursue career advancement.

Baldwin, Allgrunn, and Ring (2011) extend this work by estimating elasticities on the intensive margin for primary and secondary earners in dual earner couples using one percent samples of the Census in 1980, 1990, and 2000. They find that the own-wage elasticity of primary earners is greater than that of secondary earners in 1980 and 1990 and much greater than the elasticity for husbands and wives in all three years. Their results suggest that primary and secondary earner status may be more useful than that earner's sex in categorizing the marginal worker.

In general, workers are probably more aware of their actual or potential salary or wage rate than their actual or potential tax rate when changing work status. The potential tax rate in particular requires knowledge not only of earnings of the spouse and the couple's unearned income, but also sufficient knowledge of applicable federal and state tax law. Using changes in tax rates from the Tax Reform Act of 1986, Eissa (2002) finds that high-income married women had participation elasticities with respect to after-tax wages of 0.4 using data from the CPS. Eissa and Hoynes (2004) examine the response of lower-income married men and women to changes in the earned income tax credit. Using data from the March CPS from 1985 through 1997, they examine the response of primary earners (defined to be men) and secondary earners (defined to be women) in a couple. They estimate that primary earners have participation elasticities with respect to after-tax wages of 0.03 while secondary earners have an elasticity of 0.27.

Heim (2009) uses the 2001 wave of the Panel Study of Income Dynamics (PSID) to estimate a structural model of labor supply and the effects of taxation. As in his previous work, Heim estimates elasticities for married women that are lower than most other estimates. For example, the female participation elasticity with respect to after-tax wages is in the range of 0.07 to 0.18. He also finds, unusually, that the intensive margin elasticities exceed the extensive margin elasticities. In an unpublished appendix, Heim analyzes potential reasons for the difference between these estimates and higher numbers found in other research.

Using the 1986 and 2001 waves of the PSID, he shows that a failure to account for heterogeneity causes a substantial increase in estimated elasticities.

A related literature uses changes in tax rates to estimate the elasticity of taxable income. This elasticity captures labor supply responses and changes in productivity and income timing. Gruber and Saez (2002) use a panel of tax data from 1979 through 1990 to estimate the effect of changes over time in the net-of-tax rate and after-tax income on the change in pre-tax broad income (a measure of gross income before adjustments). While the response to tax rates in this analysis includes more than participation responses, many subsequent papers which use tax data, including our own, use similar methods (see Gruber, Slemrod, and Giertz 2012 for a review). They exploit changes in federal and state tax rates over time and across the income distribution, but note that the net-of-tax rate is endogenously determined by pre-tax income. To address that endogeneity, they instrument for the change in the net-of-tax rate by applying the second period tax rules to first period income, assuming real income is constant between periods. As a result, changes in the simulated net-of-tax rate are due solely to changes in tax rates and not income. Because the first period income itself might be endogenous, they add a ten-piece spline of first period income as a set of control variables. In their preferred specification, they estimate an elasticity of income with respect to the net-of-tax rate of 0.07.

3. Empirical Framework

In this section we describe our data and our analyses. We conduct a descriptive analysis of work participation patterns in our panel and a regression analysis to isolate the effect of tax rate changes on work.

3.1 Data

Our analysis uses panel data derived from federal individual income tax returns from 1999 to 2010, drawn from a sample of filers in 1999 and stratified by income (see Weber and Bryant 2005). The panel contains data from 931,836 tax returns belonging to 118,877 unique tax units, of which 52,452 are couples filing jointly. We observe data on wages derived from the W-2 and data on income derived from Schedules C, F, and SE for each spouse. In addition, the Social Security Administration provides date of birth and sex information that is matched to each taxpayer by Social Security number. In some cases where the sex is unknown, the IRS staff edits the information if the sex of the spouse is known or by examining the name of the taxpayer. Records are weighted to be representative of filers in 1999.

We restrict our sample to focus on labor supply responses to tax rate changes. Only couples in which both spouses were born between 1948 and 1978 are included, in order to avoid labor supply changes associated with entering the workforce or retirement. We further restrict the sample to tax units filing jointly in 1999 for as long as the taxpayer filed jointly with the same spouse, so that labor supply changes are unrelated to changes in marital status. In the U.S., married couples have the option of filing separately, but most choose to file jointly. Filing separately can substantially raise a married couple's taxes because a number of exemptions and credits, such as the earned income tax credit, cannot be taken. In 1999, married couples filed 49.9 million joint returns and 2.4 million separate returns.

About one-quarter of the observations belonging to prime-age married taxpayers were removed because they were post-divorce or post-nonfiling. Couples in which the sex of either spouse was inconsistent or unknown were also excluded. Our final sample contains data derived from 210,904 tax returns belonging to 21,239 unique tax units. Almost two-thirds of tax units in the final sample appear in the panel for all 12 years.

3.2 Transitions Across Employment Statuses

We begin by documenting the patterns of labor force participation in our data. We define an individual as working if he or she has wages or positive self-employment income in a year. Self-employment income is measured as net earnings reported on Schedule SE (the schedule for reporting self-employment tax), if one is required to be filed, or the sum of net profit or loss from up to three Schedule Cs (the schedule for reporting personally-owned businesses, such as partnerships) and Schedule Fs (the schedule for reporting farm income). Wages are aggregated from all W-2s belonging to the individual. Our definition implies that a person is counted as employed for an entire year even if he or she works for only a few hours. Thus, in our approach relatively few people become unemployed or stay unemployed, and relatively more become employed or stay employed than would be the case if labor force status was measured at a point in time.

We examine transitions into and out of work and transitions between primary and secondary earner status using the panel aspect of the data, where the primary earner in a year is defined as the spouse with higher earnings in that year. Because we observe only total earnings in a year, not wage rates or hours worked, we cannot distinguish whether an individual is working year round, full time or part time, or part of the year. For each individual, we do not determine their earnings relative to their spouse's in the first and last years of each employment spell because it is likely that an individual who stops or starts working would only have earnings during part of the year, while the spouse who continued working would have earnings from the entire year. Therefore, including partial years of work would tend to overestimate the frequency that the lower earner in a couple stops or starts working. Our restriction effectively limits our analysis of transitions to couples that have some attachment to the labor force, because at least one spouse has earnings in at least three consecutive years.

We compare the employment status and relative earnings in one year with those same variables two years later. Interesting comparisons arise from cases in which only one spouse is working in the first year, but both are working two years later. For example, when a husband works in the first year and both spouses are working two years later, we can compare their relative incomes in the later year to establish how frequently the newly-working wife outearns her husband. Of even greater interest are cases in which both members are working at time t and one member has exited the labor force two years later. By comparing exits by men, women, primary earners, and secondary earners, we can establish each group's relative attachment to the labor force.

3.3 Regression Model

We estimate the participation elasticity for three separate groups: men, women, and secondary earners. By separately estimating our model on women and secondary earners we can compare their elasticities calculated from the same data. Estimating male participation elasticities allows us to test whether those elasticities have risen along with the increase in husbands as secondary earners.

In our base model, we identify secondary earners based on a comparison of the time average of positive earnings of each spouse. On this basis, the status as secondary earner does not change over time and so it cannot be correlated with the decision to work. Under this definition, couples in which one spouse never works would not have a secondary earner.

Our estimation method uses a dynamic probit model of the following form:

$$\Pr(w_{it} = 1 \mid Y_{it}, NTR_{it}, w_{it-1}, \boldsymbol{X}_{it}, c_i) =$$
$$\Pr(\beta_1 \log(NTR_{it}) + f(\log(Y_{it})) + \rho w_{it-1} + \boldsymbol{X}_{it}\gamma + c_i + \varepsilon_{it} > 0) =$$
$$\Phi(\beta_1 \log(NTR_{it}) + f(\log(Y_{it})) + \rho w_{it-1} + \boldsymbol{X}_{it}\gamma + c_i), \tag{1}$$

where w_{it} is an indicator equal to 1 if the individual is working and NTR_{it} is the net-of-tax rate $1 - \tau_{it}$. We control for after-tax nonlabor income Y_{it} flexibly by using a 5-piece spline—defined as $f(\cdot)$ in equation (1)—based on quintiles of after-tax income. The individual's after-tax nonlabor income equals pre-tax nonlabor income minus tax liability T_{it}. Pre-tax nonlabor income is $E_{it} + U_{it}$, the sum of the spouse's earnings and the couple's unearned income. $\boldsymbol{X}_{it}$ is a vector of additional covariates, and c_i is the unobserved individual-level heterogeneity. All dollar amounts are converted into 2012 dollars using the personal consumption expenditures deflator.

6

The indicator for work, w_{it}, includes both income from self-employment and businesses and wages. Because self employment and business income is self-reported, there is a potential for underreporting of that income. As a sensitivity check, we also estimate our model where we define work and earnings solely on the basis of wages from the W-2s.

We include the age and square of age for each spouse, the number of child dependents, the number of other dependents, dummy variables for years, and the state-level unemployment rate for the appropriate sex and year obtained from the Bureau of Labor Statistics (BLS) tabulations of the CPS in our vector of covariates X_{it}. The age variables account for life cycle effects that might affect both work decisions and spousal income. The presence of dependents, especially children, is possibly endogenous. However, some studies have found that while labor force participation responds to fertility changes, the reverse effect is insignificant (McNown and Rajbhandary, 2003). We therefore assume that conditional on prior employment status and the spouse's income, fertility shocks are not affected by female labor force participation or the labor force participation of the secondary earner. The year dummy variables prevent conflating the effects of national economic conditions with those of federal tax rates. The state-level unemployment rate controls for local economic circumstances that could cause involuntary unemployment of the marginal worker. The means and standard deviations for our regression variables are presented in Table 1.

Unlike our analysis of transitions, in the regression analysis we include all observations regardless of whether they worked in at least three consecutive years. Instead, we restrict the analysis to marginal workers whose spouses have predicted earnings exceeding $100 as individuals with extremely low earnings are likely to experience mean reversion.

3.3.1 Identifying Variation in Tax Rates
To identify the effects of the net-of-tax rate on labor participation, we exploit variation in tax rates over time (see Gruber and Saez, 2002, for a discussion of this approach). A major change in the federal rate structure occurred in 2001, with an acceleration of some provisions in 2003. During the 12 years covered by the panel, 28 states changed their tax rates. Over that period, some states increased their marginal tax rates, while others lowered marginal tax rates. Giertz (2007) raises the possibility that the state rate faced by a taxpayer may be endogenous to some degree because of migration across states. To test that idea, he compares the elasticity of broad income estimated using variation in state tax rates and again using variation in federal rates over the period 1979 to 1998 and found that endogeneity due to migration has little, if any, effect on elasticity estimates.

The tax rate faced by the marginal worker can be calculated in several ways. In our main specification, we use the tax rate on the first dollar of earnings, one of the methods used in Heim (2007). This is determined by an individual's nonlabor income, defined as the sum of the spouse's earnings and the couple's unearned income. If the marginal worker is not working, it is the rate actually paid by the couple on the last dollar of earnings.

However, this rate may not be known by marginal workers who are employed. A more salient measure for those with earnings is the tax rate based on total earnings of the couple, but that rate is clearly endogenous. As an alternative, we follow Heim (2007) and use an estimate of earnings that is independent of the worker's work decision to create a measure of their tax rate. Here we use one of three estimates of the marginal worker's income: either the median annual earnings based on year and sex, the annual earnings for a full-time employee earning the minimum wage in the couple's state, or average income predicted from a regression of positive log income on spouse's income, state of residence, and demographic variables. The tax liability calculated from these alternatives is also incorporated into the after-tax nonlabor income used in the sensitivity checks.

We calculate marginal tax rates and total taxes based on federal and state income taxes using the NBER TAXSIM program. In Table 2, we describe the variation in the first dollar net-of-tax rate faced by women and secondary earners across time and quintiles based on after-tax nonlabor income. Because of the progressive tax code, the net-of-tax rate, on average, decreases as income increases. The net-of-tax rate tends to increase over time, particularly among individuals in the higher income quintiles. Outside of the bottom quintile, the average net-of-tax rate using alternative constructions of the tax rate is similar to the average first-dollar net-of-tax rate.

If the spouse's income is endogenous, then the tax rate will be endogenous as well. For example, there could be simultaneous shocks to both the work decision and the spouse's income, or a spouse could increase his or her income in response to an unemployment shock. If earned income can be written as $E_{it} = \delta E_{it-1} + \eta_{it}$, this would imply that η_{it} and ε_{it} are correlated. To address this issue, we use a method similar to that used by Gruber and Saez (2002) and Giertz (2007) to create instruments: we apply a fixed growth rate to earnings from a prior year. We index the spouse's earnings from the previous year (E_{it-1}) by the growth rate of median weekly earnings by sex and state. Thus, predicted earnings $\widehat{E_{it}}$ equals $g_{it} \times E_{it-1}$, where g_{it} is one plus the growth rate of weekly median earnings obtained from tabulations by the BLS of the Current Population Survey (CPS).

Unearned income includes dividends, interest, and rent. Because of possible endogeneity, we omit unemployment insurance. Capital gains are excluded because gains realizations are volatile and unlikely

8

to be related to labor force participation. Unearned income does not enter the model separately, which implies a unitary model of marriage (Rosen 1976, Heim 2007) rather than the collective model (Chiappori 1988). While the collective model is desirable in some applications, here it would force us to arbitrarily allocate taxes and deductions between earned and unearned income.

We estimate a dynamic model that includes w_{it-1} to account for the possibility that employment occurs in spells. Without w_{it-1}, our estimates will be biased because ε_{it} and ε_{it-1} would be correlated, and from above η_{it-1} and ε_{it-1} are correlated, and so η_{it-1} and ε_{it} are correlated. Thus, the prior year's work status would be correlated with both the dependent variable w_{it} and Y_{it}, leading to inconsistent estimation of the effect of NTR_{it}.

Even after controlling for w_{it-1}, it is possible that NTR_{it} is endogenous if E_{it-1} is endogenous. Gruber and Saez (2002) address a similar endogenity of their instrument by adding pretax income at *t-1* as a control variable. Our model controls for income by including a measure of after-tax nonlabor income Y_{it}, which is a function of E_{it-1} both through the pretax income measure and the tax liability T_{it}. In the set of linear models below we include a sensitivity test that separately estimates the effect of pretax income ($\widehat{E_{it}} + U_{it}$) and the tax liability.

3.3.2 Additional Estimation Issues
Because unobserved heterogeneity can upwardly bias elasticity estimates (Heim 2009), we model c_i as a correlated random effect:

$$c_i = \alpha_0 + \bar{\mathbf{Z}}_i \boldsymbol{\alpha_1} + \alpha_2 w_{i0} + a_i, \text{ where } a_i \sim N(0, \sigma_a^2), \mathbf{Z}_i = \{\mathbf{Z}_{i1}, \mathbf{Z}_{i2}, \dots, \mathbf{Z}_{iT}\}, \mathbf{Z}_{it} = [NTR_{it}, \mathrm{f}(Y_{it}), \mathbf{X}_{it}],$$

and $\bar{\mathbf{Z}}_i$ is the time average of each element of $\mathbf{Z}_{it}$ (Wooldridge 2010b). We address the initial conditions problem using the method presented in Wooldridge (2010). That solution assumes that the distribution of c_i is conditional on w_{i0}, which we implement by adding w_{i0} as a control variable.

Although dynamic probit models were developed for balanced panels and our regression sample is unbalanced because individuals exit the sample when they stop filing or get divorced, we can still estimate our model consistently if conditional on our explanatory variables, the distribution of c_i is independent of the number of times the individual is observed. We follow Wooldridge's (2010b) method to account for our unbalanced panel by interacting the number of years the individual is in the sample, T_i, with the time averages $\bar{\mathbf{Z}}_i$ and including a set of indicators for the number of years the individual is observed. The variance is modeled as a function of the number of years the individual is in the sample, which partially accounts for differences across individuals who are in the sample for different lengths of time.

9

We calculate the average partial effect of covariate j as

$$APE_j = \hat{\beta}_j \sum_{i=1}^{N} p_i \phi \left(\frac{Z_t \hat{\beta} + \sum \hat{\psi}_r 1[T_i = r] + \sum 1[T_i = r] \overline{Z_t} \hat{\vartheta}_r}{\exp(\sum 1[T_i = r] \hat{\omega}_r)^{1/2}} \right) \qquad (2)$$

where p_i are stratification weights such that $\sum p_i = 1$, $\hat{\omega}_r$ is the estimated variance for individuals in the sample r years, and $\hat{\beta}_j$ is the estimated coefficient from a heteroskedastic probit. The function $1[T_i = r]$ is equal to one when $T_i = r$ and 0 otherwise.

We estimate equation (1) using clustered standard errors and use the delta method to calculate the standard error of the associated *APE*. For each group—men, women, and secondary earner—we estimate the elasticities of interest, those of the net-of-tax rate and nonlabor income, as

$$elasticity_j = \frac{APE_j}{\sum_{i=1}^{N} p_i 1[w_{it} = 1]} \qquad (3)$$

To examine the effects of our assumptions we use a linear probability model. We begin by estimating a model on pooled data:

$$w_{it} = \beta_0 + \beta_1 \log(NTR_{it}) + \beta_2 \log(Y_{it}) + X_{it}\gamma + \varepsilon_{it} \qquad (4)$$

After estimating this naïve model, we include additional complexity in our model. We control for unobserved heterogeneity by separately estimating a fixed effect model and a model with w_{it-1} as an explanatory variable. We consider heterogeneous income effects by using a five-piece spline based on quintiles and also by applying stratification weights. Although fixed effects and the lagged endogenous variable both control for many unobserved characteristics, using both also allows us to control for possible serial correlation in work status.

We examine whether the effect of the net-of-tax rate or nonlabor income differs across the income distribution. Simply pooling together observations from different income groups can upwardly bias the estimated elasticity of women if wives have a greater tendency to not work as their husband's earnings increase. Controlling for a wife's nonlabor income addresses this problem to some degree because that includes her husband's earnings. However, if the effect is nonlinear in income—so that wives of high-income husbands respond differently than those with lower-income husbands—the response could be attributed to NTR_{it}, which is a nonlinear function of income. For women and secondary earners separately, we rank individuals by the average after-tax nonlabor available to them during the panel and categorize them into quintiles. For each quintile, we estimate equation 1 but include the log of after-tax income without a spline.

Another potential concern is our identification of the secondary earner. We define the secondary worker as the spouse whose average earnings over the years he or she works is lower. But if the distribution of earnings is sufficiently skewed, it is possible that a person is designated as the secondary earner even if he or she has greater earnings than his or her spouse in most years. We use three alternative definitions of secondary earner in robustness checks. First, we identify the secondary earner as the spouse with lower earnings in 75 percent or more of the years he or she is observed. Under this definition, a spouse who never works would be classified as the secondary earner. Second, we project the log of earnings on indicators for state, year, sex, number of dependent children, age, and age squared for men and women separately using full years of work. We then calculate predicted earnings for each spouse and identify the secondary earner as the spouse with lower projected earnings. Third, we identify the secondary earner as the spouse with lower relative earnings two years ago, with earnings from two years ago imputed with earnings from three years ago if the individual worked for a partial year two years ago. This provides a comparison with the analysis of transitions in and out of the work, but it can produce inconsistent estimates because a person will not be the secondary earner in a given year—and so will not be in the dataset—if the earner experiences a large positive wage shock.

4. Results and Discussion

4.1 Stylized Facts

Wives earned more than their husbands in about 21 percent of couples in 1999. We categorize couples into quintiles based on the couple's total earnings to examine how the share of women who outearn their husbands varies across the income distribution. In the bottom quintile, the wife is the sole earner in about 13 percent of couples (see Figure 1). In another 15 percent of couples, both spouses work and the wife earns more. Outside of the bottom quintile, the share of couples in which only the wife works drops sharply, as does the share of couples in which only the husband works. The most common arrangement in every quintile is that the husband is the primary earner in a two-earner couple, and the share of these households increases through the first four income quintiles. From this it appears that women are frequently the secondary earners or they are out of the labor force. If women are always the lower earner it is irrelevant if the marginal worker is determined by a person's sex or by relative income. However, there is a substantial share of dual earner couples in which the woman is the primary earner, ranging from about 15 percent in the bottom quintile to 19 percent in the fourth quintile. In the top three income quintiles, two-earner couples in which the wife is the primary earner are more common than couples in which the husband is the sole earner. Similar patterns appear if only wages are included.

To disentangle the entry and exit from the labor force by women and secondary earners, we examine transitions over two-year periods into and out of employment by sex and by relative earnings status. As described in the previous section, we exclude two-year transitions that begin or end in a year that is the first or last year of an employment spell. Therefore the analysis of transitions only counts "work" among individuals who had earnings in at least three consecutive years.

In the most common situation (44.8 percent of the transitions), both spouses worked, and the husband earned more than his wife in the initial year and two years later (see Table 3, Panel A). The next most common pattern was that the husband was the sole earner in both years (18.6 percent), followed by dual-earner couples in which the wife out-earned her husband in both years (13.7 percent). Overall, in 82 percent of cases the employment status of the couple does not change between the initial year and two years later.

This persistence also can be viewed by examining the frequency of outcomes for each initial state (see Table 3, Panel B). For two earner couples, the primary earner in the first year is usually still the primary earner two years later. If the husband is the primary earner, in 84 percent of the cases he is still the primary earner in a dual-earner couple two years later. Similarly, the wife is still the primary earner in 73 percent of the cases. However, wives who are primary earners are more likely to become secondary earners than are husbands who are primary earners. If the wife is the primary earner in the first year, in 21 percent of the cases she is the secondary earner two years later, while if the husband is the primary earner in the first year, in 10 percent of the cases he is the secondary earner two years later.

A similar pattern occurs when the sole earner in a couple is joined by his or her spouse two years later. Regardless of the sex of the sole earner in the first year, in about 12 percent of transitions the other member starts working but earns less. But if the wife is the sole worker, in 10 percent of the cases the husband starts working and becomes the primary earner. If the husband is the sole worker, in 1 percent of the cases the wife starts working and becomes the primary earner. The intuition for this asymmetry can be seen in Figure 1. When wives are the sole earner the family income is frequently in the first income quintile, while couples in which the husband is the sole earner are more evenly distributed across the quintiles. Thus, if the husband starts working and is paid the median salary for men he is very likely to become the primary earner, but if the wife starts working and is paid the median salary for women she is less likely to become the primary earner. The effect of assortative mating will alter the probabilities to the degree that taxpayers with similar incomes will tend to marry each other, but the underlying intuition remains.

When a member of a two-earner couple stops working, relative earnings play a much stronger role than the member's sex. When the female is the primary earner, the male stops working in 4.6 percent of the cases and the female stops in only 1.7 percent of the cases. If the male is the primary earner, the female stops working in 4.8 percent of the cases and the male stops in only 1.4 percent of the cases.

The predominance of relative earnings in determining which member of the couple stops working can be seen in Table 4, in which we use the results of Table 3 to examine just instances in which one member of a two-earner couple exits the labor force. If the female is the secondary worker, she is the exiting member of the couple in 77.5 percent of the cases. If the male is the secondary worker, he is the exiting member in 72.3 percent of the cases. It is clear, then, that relative earnings play a larger role than a person's sex in determining which member exits the labor force.

The exception to this pattern is when the tax unit expands from having no dependent children to claiming one or more dependent children. In that case, women are more likely to stop working than the lower earner. In dual earner couples with a female primary earner, if one member stops working, 67 percent of the time it is the woman. Among couples with a male primary earner, if one member exits it is almost always—94 percent of the time—the woman.

These results may poorly describe the greater importance of earnings if women are very infrequently in the labor force. For example, individuals who work alternating years are not tallied in our transition matrix because employment spells spanning three years are required. If those individuals are primarily women, our results will mistakenly de-emphasize the role of their gender in determining the marginal worker in a couple. As an alternative, we examine the number of years before either spouse stops working for the first time among couples who first appeared as dual earner couples in 2000 (see Figure 2).[1] Among dual earner couples with a male primary earner, in about 80 percent of couples the husband worked continuously since 2000 (only 20 percent have stopped working for at least a year), while only about 42 percent of these couples have a wife continuously working (about 58 percent have stopped working for at least a year). Those results would be consistent with women being the marginal worker in the household. But among couples in which the wife is the primary earner, the male secondary earner is more likely to stop working sooner than the female primary earner. Again, while the member's sex appears to play a role, the relative earnings of the husband and wife play a larger role.

---

[1] The hazard rates decline in some years because couples leave the sample after they get divorced or stop filing.

4.2 Regression Results

We begin by estimating equation (1) for women and men separately (see Table 5). For women, employment status in the prior year is positive and statistically significant, as expected. Increases in one's own age or the age of one's spouse decreases the probability of work, conditional on other variables. The coefficient on unemployment is positive, but statistically insignificant. The coefficient on log (NTR) is 0.13 and is statistically significant, with a z score of 2.56. Some of the spline variables for income are statistically significant, though the direction of their effect is counterintuitive. Children and other dependents decrease the probability that a woman works, though only the number of children has a statistically significant effect. For men, previous employment status is a strong determinant for working in the current period. Unlike the case for women, both the number of children and the number of other dependents are positive but statistically insignificant.

Calculating the average partial effect, a 1 unit increase in the log of the net-of-tax rate increases the probability that a woman works by 1.8 percentage points, on average (see Table 6). The woman's nonlabor income, or the household income assuming she does not work, has virtually no effect on the likelihood that she works and is statistically insignificant. We would expect nonlabor income to have a negative effect—marginal workers in couples with additional resources would be less likely to work—but we generally do not find evidence of this. When we expand our sample to include all women without restrictions based on her spouse's predicted earnings, our estimates of the average partial effects are essentially the same.

For men, changes in the net-of-tax rate and nonlabor income have statistically and economically insignificant effects on their work decisions. The low responsiveness of men's labor supply participation with respect to tax rates and income is consistent with previous estimates using survey data. Almost all— 93 percent—of prime-age men work in years of our panel. A substantial number have wives with no or very low predicted earnings, so restricting the regression to men whose wives had predicted earnings above $100 effectively limits the sample to men with after-tax nonlabor income in the second quintile and above.

For secondary workers—those with relatively lower average earnings conditional on working—a 1 unit increase in the log net-of-tax rate results in a 2.6 percentage point increase in the probability of work. While this effect is small, it is still statistically significant. The effect of income is essentially zero and is statistically insignificant.

These estimates translate into participation elasticities with respect to the net-of-tax rate of 0.004 for men, 0.023 for married women, and 0.033 for secondary workers (see Table 7). This result is consistent with our descriptive analysis, which shows that secondary earners are more likely to enter and leave the workforce than are women. In other words, being the secondary earner is a more important determinant of exit than a person's sex. While secondary workers have slightly higher elasticities with respect to tax rates than women, both of these elasticities are fairly low. This suggests that women and men, whether they are the primary or secondary earners, have a strong attachment to the labor force or are completely separated from it. To the extent that workers choose to enter or leave employment, tax rates do not strongly affect that decision. Our low estimated participation elasticities also suggest that changes in taxable income in response to changes in tax rates (Gruber and Saez 2002; Saez, Slemrod, and Giertz 2012) are not likely to be driven by participation changes among the marginal worker in a couple.

Our estimated elasticities are smaller than estimates in most of the literature, although they are similar in magnitude to wage elasticities in Heim (2007). Because the wage rates are likely to be more salient than net-of-tax rates, we expect the net-of-tax rate elasticities should be no higher than the elasticity with respect to wages. In addition, the first dollar net-of-tax rate may not be as salient as a tax rate that is based on earnings for individuals who work. We examine whether our low elasticities are the result of using the tax rate on the first dollar of the earnings of a potential worker. However, our three alternative tax rate measures that account for those earnings produce even smaller elasticities (see Table 8). This suggests that our low elasticities are not driven by the construction of the marginal tax rate variable.

Heim (2009) attributes much of the difference between the higher estimates in the existing literature and his lower estimates to his accounting for heterogeneity and using data from more recent years. We explore the possibility that our assumptions—in particular, the use of the correlated random effects model—contribute to our low estimates by estimating several linear models. We start by estimating the elasticity of the net-of-tax rate with a linear probability model applied to the pooled data, with the log of income entering as a simple continuous variable rather than as a spline. The estimated elasticity is 0.40 for women and 0.21 for secondary workers (see Table 9). This substantially higher elasticity for women is consistent with some earlier estimates of participation elasticities.

Next, we account for heterogeneity by adding previous employment status as an explanatory variable. In a pooled model, this acts as a proxy variable that controls for features that previously affected the work decision, including omitted characteristics that vary over time and others that are relatively fixed. The resulting elasticities drop to 0.09 for women and 0.08 for secondary earners.

Alternatively, we account for heterogeneity in income responses by adding a five-piece spline for income. Again, the elasticities of 0.07 and 0.05 are substantially below those from the simple pooled model.

Adding a lagged work status variable reduces the elasticities even further, to 0.03 for both women and secondary earners.

However, because we have panel data we can estimate these same models by directly accounting for unobserved heterogeneity using individual fixed effects. First, we estimate a fixed-effects model without a lag for work status or a spline for income. The elasticity for women drops to 0.05 and the elasticity for secondary workers drops to 0.07, strongly suggesting that failing to account for unobserved propensities to work led to the higher estimates. Adding lagged employment status to account for variables that previously affected employment status but that are not fixed over time results in elasticities of 0.03 and 0.05. Estimating a fixed-effects model with a spline also results in elasticities of 0.03 and 0.05 for women and secondary earners, respectively. Finally, we include both the lagged employment status and an income spline in a fixed-effects model, and the elasticities of 0.02 and 0.04 are identical to those found in our dynamic probit model. Although not shown in the table, estimated elasticities using our three alternative measures of marginal tax rates are nearly identical—between 0.02 and 0.03 for women and between 0.02 and 0.04 for secondary workers.

We also use stratification weights as a simple check for correct specification of our model. In a properly specified model, weighting observations based on an explanatory variable will not affect the estimates. If more heavily weighted observations within particular ranges of an explanatory variable change the elasticities, the model may be mis-specified. Applying weights to the pooled model without lagged employment status or an income spline reduces the elasticity for women to 0.15, suggesting that the model is mis-specified. Applying weights to the fixed effects model with lagged employment and a spline for income does not affect the estimates at one significant digit.

Finally, we use the linear model to examine two additional issues. When we model the work decision by allowing current work status to depend on past work status, we allow for a more complex error structure using first an AR (1) and then ARMA (1,1) processes. The estimated elasticities are similar to estimates from the dynamic probit. We also model work as a function of pre-tax nonlabor income and tax liability separately, so that pre-tax income can control for potential endogeneity in the net-of-tax rate. Estimated elasticities from that specification are also similar to the basic results using the dynamic probit.

Our estimated elasticities are similar in magnitude to Heim's (2007) estimates of a potential worker's participation elasticity with respect to her own wages, although the methodology differs in two ways. First, we only use changes in participation with respect to net-of-tax rates, rather than pre-tax or after-tax wages. Second, we include self-employed individuals in our analysis, while they are excluded in most analyses using survey data because of data issues. However, if we only include wages in our definition of work and income, our estimated elasticities of participation with respect to the net-of-tax rate and income remain unchanged for men and are about 0.03 for women and for secondary workers (see Table 10).

We test whether participation elasticities vary across the income distribution. For women and secondary earners, the elasticity with respect to the net-of-tax rate is lower in the first three nonlabor income quintiles and higher in the top two quintiles, though it peaks in the fourth quintile (see Figure 3). All of the elasticities are less than 0.1 and the elasticities with respect to income among women and secondary earners are much smaller.

In our main specification, the secondary earner in the household is the spouse with lower average earnings, based on the years he or she is working. Our elasticity estimates are robust to alternative definitions of the secondary earner. The responsiveness of work participation to changes in the net-of-tax rate is comparable whether the secondary earner is defined on the basis of having lower average earnings or lower projected earnings (see Table 11). If, however, the secondary worker is defined on the basis of having lower earnings in 75 percent of the years the couple is observed in the panel, the decision to work is substantially more responsive to changes in the tax rate—a 1 unit increase in the log of the net-of-tax rate increases the share who work by 4.6 percent. Two factors contribute to the higher elasticity using this definition of secondary earner—first, the estimated average partial effect is slightly higher compared to other definitions, and second, a lower share of secondary earners in this group work. Nevertheless, the elasticities are still much lower than found in much of the literature.

5. Conclusion

We use panel data derived from federal income tax returns and information returns to examine work participation patterns and estimate the elasticity of participation with respect to the net-of-tax rate for women and secondary earners. While administrative data has some advantages over survey data for measuring tax rates and work participation, there are also some limitations. Work is defined on the basis of having positive wages or self-employment income in a year, so our definition of unemployed is stringent.

In our data, the frequency with which women are the primary earner in two-earner couples is relatively constant across income quintiles. The frequency with which a member of a couple exits the work force is much more closely related to the relative earnings than the person's sex: over 70 percent of the exits are by the lower earner, regardless of sex. This indicates that the marginal worker is frequently the secondary earner. Our analysis of transitions is limited to couples in which at least one spouse had earnings in at least three consecutive years to enable us to determine who is the primary earner based on earnings when working the entire year. This sample restriction is likely to exclude individuals with a weak attachment to the labor force—for example, individuals who have earnings every other year would not be included— and possibly overstate the extent to which people remain in the same work status over two-year periods. However, an analysis of the length of time before an individual stops working for all two-earner couples in the initial year confirms that secondary earners of both sexes stop working sooner than primary earners of either sex.

We use a dynamic probit model to estimate the participation elasticity for married women and for secondary earners, defined as the spouse with the lower average earnings when he or she works. Using our preferred specification, we estimate a participation elasticity with respect to the net-of-tax rate of 0.02 for married women and 0.03 for secondary earners. These elasticities, while statistically significant, are smaller than most other estimates of elasticities with respect to wages. Participation elasticities with respect to income for both women and secondary earners are extremely low—they are generally below 0.001 and are statistically insignificant. Our results are robust to alternate methods for identifying the secondary earner in a couple. Other measures of the net-of-tax rate, which incorporate an individual's potential earnings, yield extremely small and statistically insignificant elasticity estimates.

We estimate a series of simple linear models to determine which assumptions contribute to our low estimated participation elasticities. The simplest model results in elasticity estimates consistent with much of the previous literature. We find that accounting for heterogeneity in taxpayer responses—either through using a fixed effects model, including a spline for income, employing stratification weights, or including lagged work status—substantially reduces estimated elasticities with respect to the net-of-tax rate.

References

Baldwin, Alex, Michael Allgrunn, and Raymond Ring, 2011, *International Journal of Applied Economics*, vol. 8, no. 1, pp. 46–54.

Blau, Francine D. and Lawrence M. Kahn, 2007, "Changes in the Labor Supply Behavior of Married Women: 1980–2000," *Journal of Labor Economics* vol. 25, no. 3, pp. 393–438.

Bureau of Labor Statistics, 2014, "Wives who earn more than their husbands, 1987–2012." Accessed August 4, 2014, www.bls.gov/cps/wives_earn_more.htm.

Eissa, Nada, 2002, *Taxation and Labor Supply of Married Women: the Tax Reform Act of 1986 as a Natural Experiment*, Working Paper No. 5023 (National Bureau of Economic Research). Accessed September 4, 2014, http://www.nber.org/papers/w5023.

Eissa, Nada and Hilary Williamson Hoynes, 2004, "Taxes and the Labor Market Participation of Married Couples: the Earned Income Tax Credit," *Journal of Public Economics* vol. 88, pp. 1931–1958.

Chiappori, Pierre-Andre, 1988, "Nash-bargained Household Decisions: A Comment," *International Economic Review,* vol. 29, pp. 791–796.

Giertz, Seth, 2007, The Elasticity of Taxable Income over the 1980s and 1990s, *National Tax Journal,* vol. 60, no. 4, pp. 743–768.

Gruber, Jon and Emmanuel Saez, 2002, "The Elasticity of Taxable Income: Evidence and Implications," *Journal of Public Economics,* vol. 84, pp. 1–32.

Heim, Bradley T., 2007, "The Incredible Shrinking Elasticities: Married Female Labor Supply, 1978–2002," *The Journal of Human Resources*, vol. 42, no. 4, pp. 881–918.

Heim, Bradley T., 2009, "Structural Estimation of Family Labor Supply with Taxes," *The Journal of Human Resources,* vol. 44, no. 2.

McNown, Robert and Sameer Rajbhandary, 2003, "Time Series Analysis of Fertility and Female Labor Market Behavior," *Journal of Population Economics,* vol. 16, pp. 501–523.

Rosen, Harvey S., 1976, "Taxes in a Labor Supply Model with Joint Wage-Hours Determination," *Econometrica,* vol. 44, no. 3, pp. 485–507.

Saez, Emmanuel, Joel Slemrod, and Seth H. Giertz, 2012, "The Elasticity of Taxable Income with Respect to Marginal Tax Rates: A Critical Review," *Journal of Economic Literature,* vol. 50, no. 1, pp. 3–50.

Shafer, Emily Fitzgibbons, 2011, "Wives' Relative Wages, Husbands' Paid Work Hours, and Wives' Labor-Force Exit," *Journal of Marriage and Family,* vol. 73, pp. 250–263.

Weber, Michael E. and Victoria L. Bryant, 2005, "The 1999 Individual Income Tax Return Edited Panel," Statistics of Income Working Papers (Internal Revenue Service). Accessed May 8, 2014, www.irs.gov/pub/irs-soi/05weber.pdf.

Wooldridge, Jeffrey M., 2010 (second edition), *Econometric Analysis of Cross Section and Panel Data,* (Cambridge, Mass.: MIT Press, 2010).

Wooldridge, Jeffrey M., 2010b, *Correlated Random Effects Models with Unbalanced Panels,* (unpublished manuscript). Accessed September 4, 2014, http://econ.msu.edu/faculty/wooldridge/docs/cre1_r4.pdf.

Figure 1
Share of joint filers in each work status, by earnings quintile, 1999

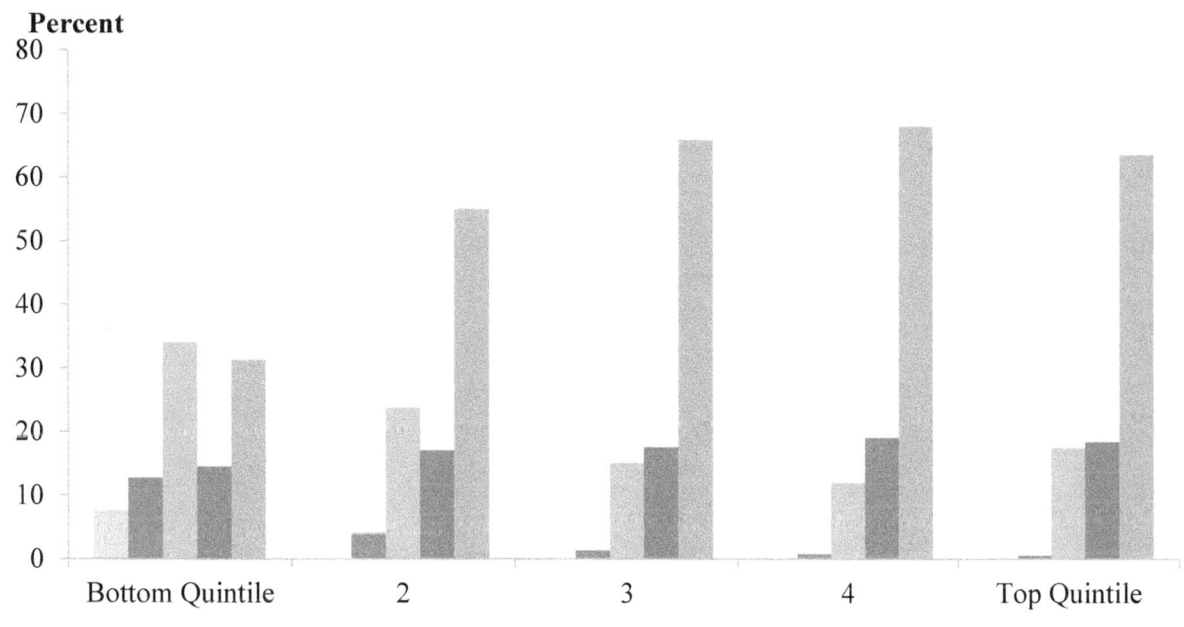

Notes: Observations weighted to be representative of the filing population in 1999. Earnings includes wages and positive self-employment income.

Figure 2

Probability that spouse in dual earner couple exits by year, by sex and relative earnings status of exiting spouse

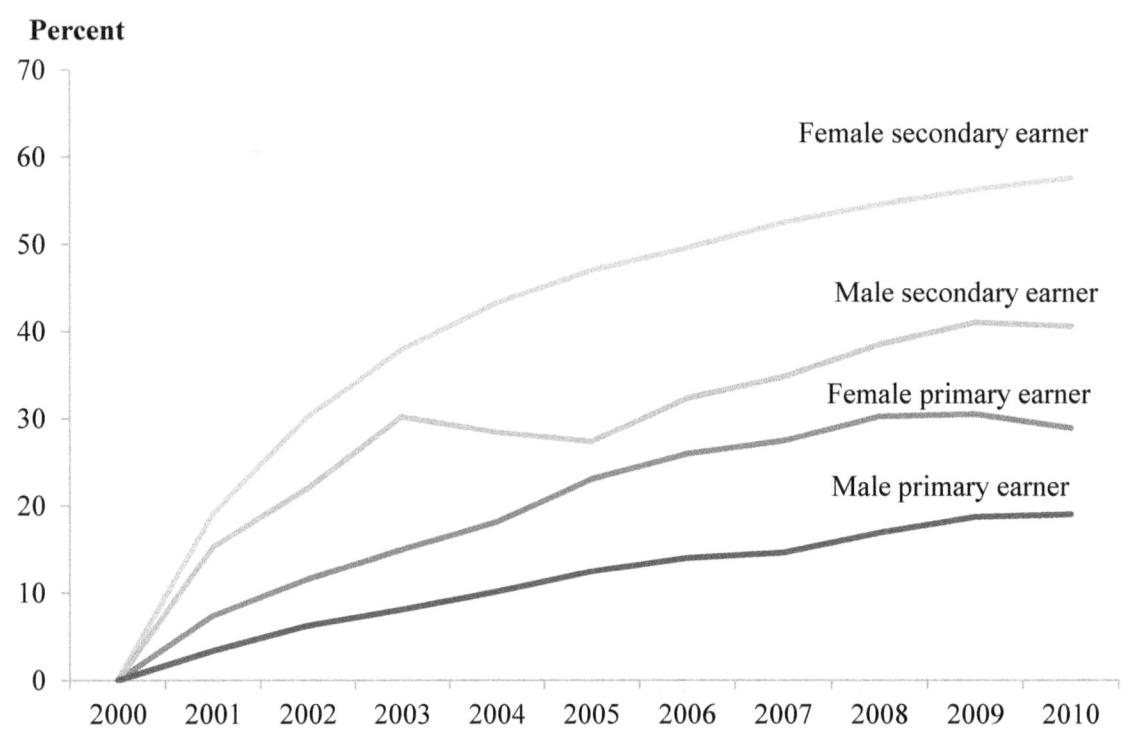

Notes: Sample consists of couples in which both spouses worked in 2000. Relative earnings status based on wages and positive self-employment income in 2000.

Figure 3
Elasticities of work, by income quintile

Panel A. Elasticity with respect to net-of-tax rate

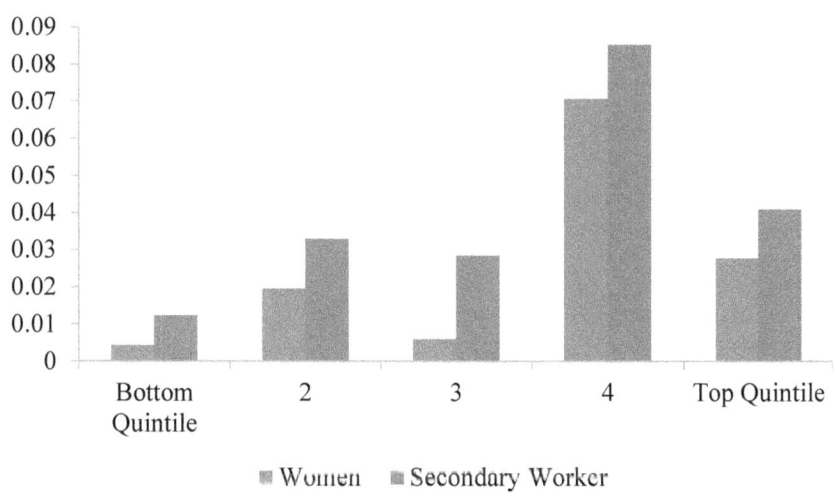

Panel B. Elasticity with respect to after-tax nonlabor income

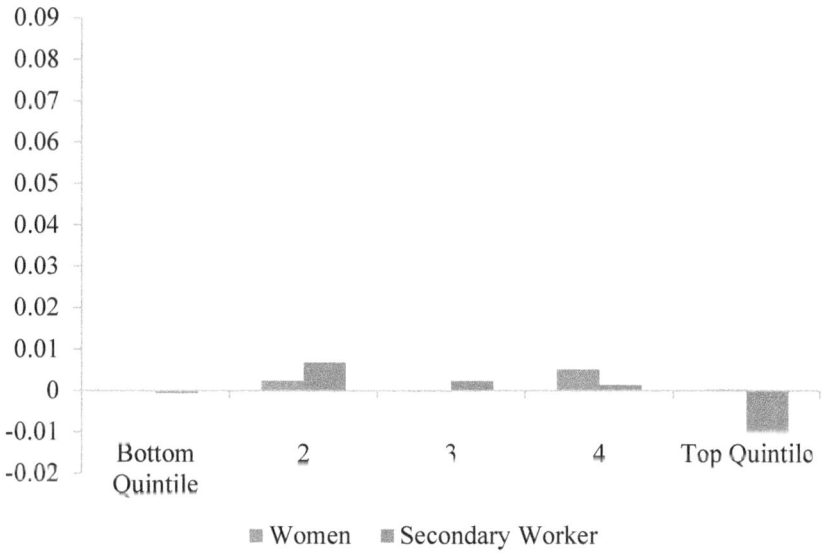

Table 1

Summary statistics of individuals in dataset

Variable	Mean	Standard Deviation
Log (first dollar net-of-tax rate)	4.49	0.25
Log (net-of-tax rate), using median earnings	4.35	0.12
Log (net-of-tax rate), using earnings at minimum wage	4.41	0.17
Log (net-of-tax rate), using predicted earnings	4.41	0.19
Log (after-tax nonlabor income)	8.50	4.18
Number of children	1.50	1.21
Number of other dependents	0.05	0.28
Unemployment rate	5.59	2.00
Age	43	8
Age squared	1947	702
Percent who work	85%	35%
Number of person-years	421,112	

Note: Weighted to be representative of the filing population in 1999.

Table 2

Variation in net-of-tax rate, by income quintile for selected years

Panel A. First dollar net-of-tax rate faced by women

Year	Income quintile				
	Bottom	2	3	4	Top
2000	120.37	81.05	82.07	79.52	59.90
	1,594	3,982	3,132	2,871	8,396
2005	118.11	87.68	81.85	82.25	65.93
	1,731	2,537	2,604	2,645	7,583
2010	120.59	90.16	79.61	82.70	67.68
	2,192	2,075	2,057	2,216	6,415

Panel B. First dollar net-of-tax rate faced by secondary worker

Year	Income quintile				
	Bottom	2	3	4	Top
2000	106.56	77.38	81.99	78.32	60.36
	1,743	3,510	2,773	2,465	5,800
2005	111.27	79.69	82.88	81.71	66.41
	1,396	2,300	2,383	2,436	5,533
2010	114.90	80.53	80.87	81.86	67.62
	1,740	1,733	1,917	2,097	4,795

Notes: Income quintiles based on nonlabor income of individual. Numbers in each year-income quintile cell show mean and number of observations.

Table 3

Transitions between employment statuses across two-year periods

Panel A. Share of all transitions (Percent)

	No workers	Only female works	Only male works	Both work, female primary earner	Both work, male primary earner	Row Total
				Year t+2		
Year t						
No workers	1.0	0.1	0.3	0.0	0.1	1.4
Only female works	0.1	3.5	0.1	0.6	0.4	4.6
Only male works	0.4	0.1	18.6	0.3	2.5	22.0
Both work, female primary earner	0.0	0.9	0.3	13.7	3.9	18.8
Both work, male primary earner	0.1	0.7	2.5	5.1	44.8	53.2

Panel B. Share of transitions, by initial state (Percent)

	No workers	Only female works	Only male works	Both work, female primary earner	Both work, male primary earner	Row Total
				Year t+2		
Year t						
No workers	67.6	6.3	19.0	2.0	5.1	100
Only female works	2.4	74.8	1.3	12.0	9.5	100
Only male works	1.8	0.4	84.8	1.4	11.6	100
Both work, female primary earner	0.2	4.6	1.7	72.8	20.7	100
Both work, male primary earner	0.2	1.4	4.8	9.5	84.1	100

Note: Work is defined by the presence of wages or positive self-employment income, weighted to be representative of filers.

Table 4

Share of exiting workers among dual earner couples, by relative earnings and sex

Sex of secondary earner	Sex of exiting worker	
	Male	Female
Male	72.3	27.7
Female	22.5	77.5

Notes: Work is defined by the presence of wages or positive self-employment income. Observations are weighted to be representative of the 1999 filing population.

Table 5
Estimated probit coefficients on probability of working

Covariate	Women (1)	Men (2)	Secondary Worker (3)
Worked in last year	0.128	0.053	0.162
	(0.050)	(0.063)	(0.054)
Worked in 1999	0.0002	n.a.	0.004
	(0.005)		(0.005)
log (net-of-tax rate)	0.008	-0.003	0.008
	(0.004)	(0.006)	(0.004)
log (after-tax income), 1st quintile	0.008	-0.006	0.007
	(0.004)	(0.005)	(0.004)
log (after-tax income), 2nd quintile	0.006	-0.004	0.003
	(0.003)	(0.005)	(0.004)
log (after-tax income), 3rd quintile	0.003	-0.006	0.001
	(0.003)	(0.005)	(0.004)
log (after-tax income), 4th quintile	2.395	2.365	2.175
	(0.016)	(0.032)	(0.015)
log (after-tax income), 5th quintile	0.496	0.632	0.206
	(0.013)	(0.03)	(0.014)
Age	0.031	0.023	0.065
	(0.058)	(0.043)	(0.088)
Age square	-0.001	-0.0005	-0.001
	(0.0002)	(0.0003)	(0.0002)
Age of spouse	-0.062	-0.248	-0.088
	(0.03)	(0.083)	(0.037)
Age of spouse squared	-0.0003	-0.0002	0.00010
	(0.0002)	(0.0003)	(0.0002)
Unemployment rate	0.0030	-0.015	-0.01
	(0.007)	(0.008)	(0.006)
Number of children	-0.033	0.02	-0.037
	(0.009)	(0.014)	(0.009)
Number of other dependents	-0.047	0.002	-0.04
	(0.03)	(0.038)	(0.029)
Mean of dependent variable	0.77	0.93	0.81
Number of observations	172,445	120,527	147,558

Notes: Standard errors clustered by individual in parentheses. Base specification excludes individuals whose spouses have predicted earnings below $100. All regressions include year dummies and heterogeneity projected on time averages of all explanatory variables. Work is defined as the presence of wages or positive self-employment income.

Table 6

Average partial effects on probability of working

Covariate	Women (1)	Men (2)	Secondary Worker (3)
log (net-of-tax rate)	0.018	0.004	0.0260
	(0.007)	(0.01)	(0.008)
log (after-tax income), 1st quintile	0.00003	n.a.	0.0010
	(0.001)		(0.001)
log (after-tax income), 2nd quintile	0.0010	-0.0002	0.0010
	(0.001)	(0.001)	(0.001)
log (after-tax income), 3rd quintile	0.0010	-0.0005	0.0010
	(0.001)	(0.001)	(0.001)
log (after-tax income), 4th quintile	0.0010	-0.0003	0.0010
	(0.001)	(0.001)	(0.001)
log (after-tax income), 5th quintile	0.0005	-0.0004	0.0002
	(0.0005)	(0.001)	(0.001)
Mean of dependent variable	0.768	0.931	0.806
Number of observations	172,445	120,527	147,558

Notes: Standard errors calculated using delta method in parentheses. Base specification excludes individuals whose spouses have predicted earnings below $100. All regressions include lagged work status, work status in 1999, age and age squared for both spouses, number of children, number of other dependents, year dummies, and state unemployment rates. Work is defined as the presence of wages or positive self-employment income.

Table 7

Elasticity of work participation

	Women (1)	Men (2)	Secondary Worker (3)
Net-of-tax rate	0.023	0.004	0.033
After-tax income, 1st quintile	0.00004	n.a.	0.001
After-tax income, 2nd quintile	0.001	-0.0002	0.002
After-tax income, 3rd quintile	0.002	-0.0005	0.001
After-tax income, 4th quintile	0.001	-0.0003	0.001
After-tax income, 5th quintile	0.001	-0.0005	0.0003

Note: Work participation is defined as having wages or positive self-employment income in a year.

Table 8

Elasticity of work participation, using different measures of own earnings

Panel A. Median earnings

	Women (1)	Men (2)	Secondary Worker (3)
Net-of-tax rate	0.015	0.030	0.021
After-tax income, 1st quintile	0.00086	0.0016	0.002
After-tax income, 2nd quintile	0.001	0.0011	0.001
After-tax income, 3rd quintile	0.001	0.0007	0.002
After-tax income, 4th quintile	0.001	0.0008	0.001
After-tax income, 5th quintile	0.001	0.0008	0.0004

Panel B. Earnings at minimum wage

	Women (1)	Men (2)	Secondary Worker (3)
Net-of-tax rate	-0.002	0.002	0.001
After-tax income, 1st quintile	0.00098	0.0011	0.003
After-tax income, 2nd quintile	0.001	0.0009	0.001
After-tax income, 3rd quintile	0.001	0.0003	0.002
After-tax income, 4th quintile	0.001	0.0002	0.001
After-tax income, 5th quintile	0.000	-0.0001	-0.0005

Panel C. Predicted earnings

	Women (1)	Men (2)	Secondary Worker (3)
Net-of-tax rate	0.026	0.006	0.024
After-tax income, 1st quintile	-0.00096	0.0005	0.001
After-tax income, 2nd quintile	0.001	-0.0002	0.001
After-tax income, 3rd quintile	0.001	-0.0003	0.001
After-tax income, 4th quintile	0.001	0.0000	0.001
After-tax income, 5th quintile	0.001	-0.0002	0.0004

Note: Work participation is defined as having wages or positive self-employment income in a year.

Table 9

Estimated elasticities of first dollar net-of-tax rate on work status from linear probability model

Model	Log (income)	Dynamics	Women	Secondary Worker
Pooled	Continuous	No lag	0.40	0.21
Pooled	Continuous	Lag	0.09	0.08
Pooled	Spline	No lag	0.07	0.05
Pooled	Spline	Lag	0.03	0.03
FE	Continuous	No lag	0.05	0.07
FE	Continuous	Lag	0.03	0.05
FE	Spline	No lag	0.03	0.05
FE	Spline	Lag	0.02	0.04
Pooled, weighted	Continuous	No lag	0.15	0.08
FE, weighted	Spline	Lag	0.02	0.04

Notes: Clustered standard errors in parentheses. Excludes individuals whose spouses have predicted earnings below $100. All regressions include age and age squared for both spouses, number of children, number of other dependents, year dummies, and state unemployment rates. Work is defined as the presence of wages or positive self-employment income. FE=fixed effects.

Table 10

Elasticity of work participation using wages only

	Women (1)	Men (2)	Secondary Worker (3)
Net-of-tax rate	0.034	0.005	0.033
After-tax income, 1st quintile	-0.0004	n.a.	0.0018
After-tax income, 2nd quintile	0.001	-0.0002	0.001
After-tax income, 3rd quintile	0.001	0.0003	0.001
After-tax income, 4th quintile	0.001	0.001	0.001
After-tax income, 5th quintile	0.0005	0.001	0.0003

Note: Work participation is defined as having wages in a year.

Table 11

Elasticity of work participation using alternative definitions of secondary worker

	Average earnings conditional on working (1)	Lower earnings 75 percent or more of the time (2)	Projected earnings (3)	Relative earnings two years ago (4)
Net-of-tax rate	0.033	0.046	0.025	0.031
After-tax income, 1st quintile	0.001	0.0005	0.0007	0.002
After-tax income, 2nd quintile	0.002	0.002	0.002	0.002
After-tax income, 3rd quintile	0.001	0.002	0.002	0.002
After-tax income, 4th quintile	0.001	0.0008	0.001	0.001
After-tax income, 5th quintile	0.0003	0.0009	0.0006	0.001

Note: Work participation is defined as having wages or positive self-employment income in a year.